DATE DUE

DEC 18 2002	JAN 20 2016
AUG 26	
DEC 19 2012	

King George III

King George III

By Robert Green

A First Book

Franklin Watts
A Division of Grolier Publishing
New York London Hong Kong Sydney
Danbury, Connecticut

Cover collage photographs ©:Art Resource; Scala/Art Resource;
Corbis-Bettman; Photofest.

Photographs ©: Archive Photos: 19; Corbis-Bettmann: 3 bottom, 7, 9, 23; Giraudon/Art Resource: 3 top, 12, 50, 54; National Portrait Gallery, London: 31; North Wind Picture Archives: 21, 26, 29, 37, 38, 39, 41; Photofest: 43, 53; Superstock, Inc.: 11, 15, 48, 49 (National Portrait Gallery, London), 17, 32, 35, 46, 57.

Library of Congress Cataloging-in-Publication Data

Green, Robert, 1969–
King George III / by Robert Green.

p. cm.—(A First book)
Includes bibliographical references and index.
Summary: A biography of the eighteenth-century British monarch during whose reign the American colonies fought to break away and form an independent nation.
ISBN 0-531-20333-6
1. George III, King of Great Britain, 1738–1820—Juvenile literature. 2. Great Britain—History—George , 1760-1820—Juvenile literature. 3. Great Britain—Kings and rulers—Biography—Juvenile literature. 4. Great Britain—History—George III, 1760-1820.
[1. George III, King of Great Britain, 1738-1820. 2. Kings, queens, rulers, etc.]
I. Title. II. Series.
DA505.G74 1997
941.07′3—dc21 96–51190
CIP
AC

Printed in the United States of America
1 2 3 4 5 6 7 8 9 10 R 06 05 04 03 02 01 00 99 98 97

Contents

An American Visitor

After peace was concluded between the newborn United States of America and Great Britain in 1783, King George III refused to meet with an American ambassador. "I shall ever," he declared, "have a bad opinion of any Englishman who would accept of being an accredited Minister for that revolted state."

Two years later at London's St. James Palace, George controlled his temper, summoned all of his resolve, and prepared to receive John Adams in the official capacity of ambassador from the United States. This was the same

An aloof-looking King George III receives John Adams as the first U.S. ambassador to the English court.

John Adams who had, in 1776, helped Thomas Jefferson, Benjamin Franklin, and other revolutionaries draft the Declaration of Independence.

Aware of the delicacy of his mission, Adams spoke graciously. "I think myself," he declared, "more fortunate than all my fellow citizens in having the distinguished honor to stand in your Majesty's presence." Adams proclaimed that their meeting would "form an epoch in the history of England and America."

The king's nerve held. He replied with equal grace, "I will be very frank with you. I was the last to conform to the separation; but the separation having been made, and having become inevitable, I have always said, as I say now, that I would be the first to meet the friendship of the United States as an independent power."

That last part was not really true. In fact, the Revolutionary War that had resulted in the birth of the United States would irk George until his final days. "I shall never," he told a friend, "rest my head on my last pillow in peace and quiet as long as I remember the loss of my American colonies." After his death, he was remembered as "the King who lost the American colonies."

One reason that George took the loss of the American colonies so badly was that he was the first king of his royal family, the House of Hanover, to regard his

George I, the first Hanoverian king of England

duties to Great Britain as sacred. Their German upbringing, and their longing for their native country, made the two kings who preceded George III (George I and George II) ill suited to sit on the British throne.

How did these Germans become British rulers? In the early 1700s, Britain was rife with political and religious intrigues, and pretenders to the throne pressed their claims. The British needed a suitable Protestant to be king. Many of the possible candidates in Britain had connections to Catholicism, and it was feared that the throne could fall into Catholic hands. So the British turned to the minor German state of Hanover to supply a Protestant prince. That man was crowned George I of Great Britain in 1714, and his coronation began the rule of the Hanoverian kings of Great Britain.

After moving to England, however, George I developed a strong dislike for his subjects. The fact that he never bothered to learn English separated him from the workings of the British government and from most Britons—he was a foreigner in his own kingdom.

George I's son and successor, George Augustus, shared his father's contempt for all things English. This George, though, had the misfortune of being able to express his opinions in English. "No English cook could dress a dinner, no English player could act, no English coachman drive," he stated after becoming King George II in 1727. Not surprisingly, George II was loathed almost universally in England.

This dislike of George II spread to Frederick, his eldest son. At the age of thirty, Frederick, Prince of Wales (as the heir to the British throne is called), married a German named Augusta and set up residence at St. James Palace. Frederick's home soon became a rallying point for politicians who were in opposition to the elected government.

At St. James Palace, Frederick established a large family. The first of their eight children, Prince George (later George III) was born on June 4, 1738. George grew very fond of his younger brother Prince Edward. Their childhood was spent in a secluded world, separate from other

Frederick, Prince of Wales, and his sisters; the lives of those in the ruling family were privileged but isolated.

children their own age. To amuse themselves, they played games, staged plays, dressed up in costume, and danced.

By the age of six, George began to study with private tutors. He studied foreign languages, history, music, and natural history, among other things. He was a lazy

George, Prince of Wales

but serious student. Sprawling theories and complex questions eluded him, but he quickly matered the details of things. More than his studies, George liked to be outside inspecting plants, flowers, bugs, and rocks. He grew into a handsome young man with fair hair and large, blue, watery eyes that he often fixed in an unblinking stare. Unlike Edward, George was solemn and inclined to wander alone through the royal estate.

George admired the ease and grace that came naturally to Edward when he was in the company of important visitors to the palace. One visitor was John Stuart, third Earl of Bute, commonly known as Lord Bute, who was a friend to Frederick and Augusta. Lord Bute, a bright, handsome, and serious-minded Scottish aristocrat, grew close to the royal family.

In March 1751, Frederick caught cold and suddenly died, making George heir to the throne at age twelve.

He felt a profound absence after the death of his father and longed for companionship. Moreover, he lacked confidence and longed for someone to help guide him. He turned to Lord Bute, who had consoled his mother after Frederick's death. In 1756, Lord Bute became Groom of the Stole, the head of George's household. Lord Bute had the social ease and intellect that George had admired in his brother Edward. Soon Lord Bute had become not only George's Groom of the Stole, but also his tutor, friend, and mentor.

As Prince of Wales, George received more and more attention from members of Parliament, the legislative branch of England's government. They knew that one day he would hold the reins of power and they wished to win him over to their various causes. George, however, was not receptive. He had come to believe, through the guidance of his mother and Lord Bute, that politicians were "myrmidons [subordinates] of the blackest kind," and no better than despots.

Bute convinced George that he could reclaim the powers of the monarchy that had fallen by the wayside under George I and George II. This idea was reinforced by his mother's constant prodding. "George, be a king," she whispered over and over into the ear of the impressionable prince.

2

"I Glory in the Name of Briton"

George's opportunity arrived suddenly on October 25, 1760. He was crossing London's Kew Bridge on horseback when a messenger presented him with the news of his grandfather's death. At age twenty-two, George was king, and ready to try his will against the will of Parliament.

The British Parliament is comprised of the House

Royal portraits, such as this one of George III as a young king, were important pieces of propaganda, depicting the king in a strong and noble light. Because photography had not been invented, George III could control these images; he could not control other images, however, such as political cartoons, which often treated him roughly.

of Lords and the House of Commons. Unelected, titled aristocrats, known as Lords, sit in the smaller House of Lords, and elected commoners sit in the larger House of Commons. The relationship between Parliament and the monarch is defined by the examples of previous monarchs and Parliaments and by the unwritten constitution of Great Britain. Just how much power a monarch would have during his or her reign was always the subject of debate and of struggle.

George II had been content to while away his days dreaming of Hanover, leaving Parliament to govern. The leader of Parliament, the prime minister, had enjoyed an increased responsibility under the Hanoverian kings. George III sought to reverse the decline of the king's powers by forcefully exerting his will over Parliament. He was determined, as his mother had hoped, to "be a king."

In his first speech to Parliament, George tried to separate himself from his German-born predecessors. "Born and bred in this country, I glory in the name of Briton," he boasted. The statement was meant to win favor among his subjects. But like so much else that George did, the gesture was misunderstood. The powerful English members of Parliament bristled at the word "Briton," which refers to natives of the entire island of Britain, including the Scots and the Welsh. In George's day, the

The British Isles in the time of King George III

English still looked upon Scotland and Wales as backward and undeserving of recognition. Moreover, those offended by George's choice of the word "Briton" saw the hand of Bute, the Scottish lord, behind the speech.

Many government ministers thought Bute no better

than a meddler who had little practical experience at politics. But George had decided long ago to place Lord Bute in the government upon becoming king. Even the slightest hint that he would rule without Bute by his side prompted George to declare, "I should with an eye of pleasure look on retiring to some uninhabited cavern."

George looked to Bute for advice on all matters. For example, as a young man, George had fallen in love with Lady Sarah Lennox, the niece of a politician named Henry Fox. When George asked Bute if he should marry her, Bute firmly told him that he must give her up; to marry a relation of a formidable politician would place George in a compromising position. George obeyed dutifully.

After George became king, he and Lord Bute searched the *Almanach de Gotha,* a list of German aristocrats, for a suitable bride. He settled on Charlotte of Mecklenburg-Strelitz. When the girl arrived in England, he found her rather unattractive but married her anyway. He desperately wanted to have an heir to secure his family's future on the throne. That heir arrived in August 1762 and was named George (later King George IV). Fourteen children were still to come.

Turning to matters of state, George quickly fulfilled his ambition to bring Bute into the government. Together they set out to reshape government policy to their liking.

The first meeting of George and Princess Charlotte. It was not uncommon for a monarch to select a bride that he had never before seen. The wife of the king was often chosen for her royal blood over her appearance or charm.

The prime minister, William Pitt, had been waging war against the French since 1756. George viewed the war, known as the Seven Years' War, as "bloody and expensive," and he intended to bring it to an end.

William Pitt, known as the Great Commoner, was one of the most successful prime ministers that Britain had ever known. He was a tall, solitary figure who could sway members of Parliament with his tremendous speeches. He was also immensely popular with the people. Under Pitt, British interests overseas had grown considerably and trade boomed. A large merchant class was emerging from overseas trade, and merchants were profiting from the war. Technology had also advanced to the point where industry was beginning to change society. Wealth was changing hands quickly, and many people moved to cities to work in factories.

The new class of merchants, as well as many aristocrats, quickly voiced their outrage at the king's proposal to end the war. After all, many Britons enjoyed trouncing the French, their traditional rival in Europe. Their voices were expressed in the government through Pitt.

In 1763, George secured a peace by means of the Treaty of Paris. This victory, however, cost him dearly. Pitt resigned from the government and went into the

William Pitt won the nickname "The Great Commoner" for his vast popularity among the middle classes of England. The fact that Pitt drew his support directly from the people and not from the aristocracy frightened George III.

opposition, where he railed against the policies of George and Bute. George considered Pitt "the blackest of hearts" and failed to recognize the success of Pitt's administration.

The king found himself disliked by the majority of his subjects. He also discovered that Lord Bute, though willing to carry out his plans, did not carry enough support among government ministers to be an effective leader in Parliament. Bute was, in fact, getting battered. He admitted that he would gladly retire "on bread and water, and think it luxury, compared with what I suffer." George finally released him from his obligations and admitted later that Lord Bute had been "deficient in political firmness."

George then began a long career of forming and dissolving governments almost at will. He had become a political realist, willing to use politicians to achieve his aims. "Bad men," claimed George, "must be called in to govern bad men." But despite his victories over individual politicians such as Pitt, the king's popularity continued to sink. Just after the Treaty of Paris, George stumbled into a conflict with the rakish and insolent publisher John Wilkes. The incident would show George just how little support he had from his subjects.

John Wilkes came from a family of merchants made wealthy from the policies of Pitt and the increase of British trade around the world. Wilkes was a member of

John Wilkes appears before wigged magistrates of the British government during his trial of 1768.

Parliament and published a newspaper called the *North Briton,* in the pages of which he launched attacks against the king and his peace policy. Wilkes's flamboyant personality and witty attacks on the government drew a great deal of attention. He existed on the fringe of political power, but he hoped he could make enough noise to win favor among opposition politicians like Pitt.

In edition number 45 of the *North Briton,* in 1763, Wilkes's personal attacks on the king finally spurred government action. The king's ministers sued Wilkes for libel and issued a general arrest warrant for the apprehension of all those involved in writing and publishing the article. Wilkes was arrested and imprisoned in the Tower of London, but he fought back by suing the government for issuing an illegal warrant. A British court decided in favor of Wilkes. He was released, and, after a long battle, damages were paid by the government.

King George fumed. "That Devil Wilkes!" he exclaimed. Most Britons, however, disagreed with the king about Wilkes. The entire case had been highly publicized in the daily papers. The image of an innocent commoner fighting the king and his ministers for the right to express his opinions caught the public's imagination. Wilkes became a hero, and the chant of "Wilkes and Liberty!" rang out in London's streets.

Of more concern to King George was the fact that the chant "Wilkes and Liberty" had become a popular slogan in the American colonies, where the colonials were embroiled in their own dispute against the British crown.

3

America Revolts

In 1760, when George III took the throne, the thirteen American colonies stretched along the Eastern coast of North America from Massachusetts (which included what is now Maine) to Georgia.

Most Britons, including the king, considered the American colonies to be of no more importance than the British West Indies or other overseas holdings. The Americans exported natural resources to Britain and provided a market for finished products crafted in Britain. Britain, on the other hand, insured the protection of the colonists with

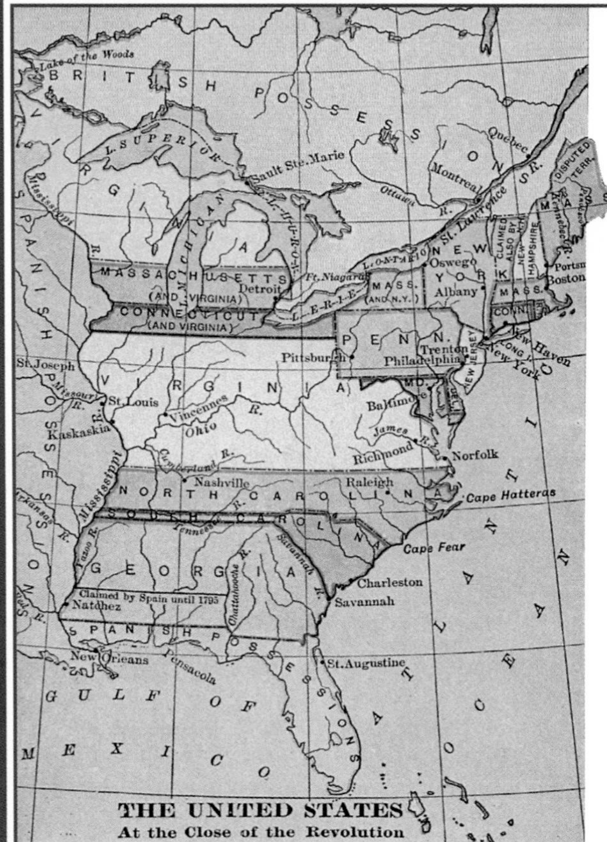

The original thirteen American states; notice that the boundaries of the states at that time stretched all the way to the Mississippi River.

its red-coated soldiery and feared naval fleet.

The rivalry among Britain, France, and Spain for control of territory in the New World drew the Americans into their first military skirmishes. Colonial forces such as the Virginia militia, commanded by a hefty six-footer named George Washington, served under British commanders in battles on American soil.

During the Seven Years' War, the number of regular British troops was increased in the colonies to prevent the French from making inroads into British territory. The British commanders and regular soldiers often scorned the less organized colonial troops. Many colonists resented their presence altogether.

The colonists were even more upset when members of Parliament decided to levy new taxes on the colonies to help pay for the British troops. The British already paid a tax on stamps for such items as newspapers and legal transactions, and it was extended to the colonies by the Stamp Act of 1765. Taxes were soon placed on tea, glass, and paper as well.

Americans had always resented British taxation, but now the issue threatened to erupt. The economy of the Americas depended primarily on trade, conducted by ship in the colonies and the West Indies. The cargo of these ships, however, was subject to taxation by the British. To avoid these taxes, colonists elevated smuggling to a national industry. Only a small percentage of the cargo carried by American ships was taxed.

Many members of Parliament felt the Americans were acting like naughty children. They determined to make the Americans pay a greater share of British debts. But this caused the Americans to unify the thirteen colonies much more tightly than before. Benjamin Franklin was chosen to plead the case in London. "No taxation without representation," he insisted.

Back in the colonies, tax collectors were being assaulted when they tried to carry out their duties, and public fervor was coming to a head. In Boston, on March

15, 1770, troops were called in to restore order. The colonists pelted the soldiers with snowballs. British troops replied with gunfire. Five colonists fell dead, and six others were wounded. This incident, now known as the Boston Massacre, drew both sides closer to war.

An illegal assembly in Massachusetts rallied the people to defiance, and similar meetings were held in Virginia and New York. In December 1773, colonists disguised as Indians boarded a British merchant ship carrying tea and dumped the 40-ton cargo into Boston's harbor.

King George and most Britons were shocked at the acts of the Americans. He still did not believe that the colonists could mount a full-scale revolt and overthrow British rule. The king referred to the Americans as "an unhappy, misled, and deluded multitude."

British policy for governing the American colonies had been mixed from the beginning. Some ministers levied taxes and others, seeing the resentment with which they were met, canceled them. The Americans became frustrated with the British government's uneven practices;

Though little blood was actually spilled, the Boston Massacre was an important rallying point for anti-British agitators, such as Paul Revere, who printed this engraving.

Unhappy BOSTON! ſee thy Sons deplore,
Thy hallow'd Walks beſmear'd with guiltleſs Gore:
While faithleſs P—n and his ſavage Bands,
With murd'rous Rancour ſtretch their bloody Hands;
Like fierce Barbarians grinning o'er their Prey,
Approve the Carnage and enjoy the Day.

If ſcalding drops from Rage from Anguiſh Wrung
If ſpeechleſs Sorrows lab'ring for a Tongue,
Or if a weeping World can ought appeaſe
The plaintive Ghoſts of Victims ſuch as theſe;
The Patriot's copious Tears for each are ſhed,
A glorious Tribute which embalms the Dead

But know FATE ſummons to that awful Goal,
Where JUSTICE ſtrips the Murd'rer of his Soul:
Should venal C—ts the ſcandal of the Land,
Snatch the relentleſs Villain from her Hand,
Keen Execrations on this Plate inſcrib'd,
Shall reach a JUDGE who never can be brib'd.

The unhappy Sufferers were Meſs.rs SAM.L GRAY, SAM.L MAVERICK, JAM.S CALDWELL, CRISPUS ATTUCKS & PAT.K CARR *Killed. Six wounded; two of them* (CHRIST.R MONK & JOHN CLARK) *Mortally*

eventually, they became resentful of Britain's rule.

The colonials blamed King George directly. He was referred to as a tyrant, or "the royal brute." But George was only following the policy of his ministers and trying to quell the revolt. In 1770, George chose Frederick, Lord North, to form a new government. In Lord North, George had found, for the first time, a minister whose views mirrored his own and who had the power to gain support for his policies in Parliament.

Lord North gave the impression of being sedated. He had a fat, calm face and enormous, sleepy eyes. His absolute calm and his charming sense of humor made him popular in the House of Commons. But above all, he was willing to defer to King George's desires. When North became prime minister, George could enter politics almost directly; always interested in the details, he instructed North on even the smallest matter.

King George, growing alarmed at the violence in America, wrote to North in 1774, "The die is now cast, the colonies must either submit or triumph. I do not wish to come to severer measures, but we must not retreat." George firmly believed that he was defending the right of Parliament to legally govern British-held territory. He was doing

Sleepy-eyed Lord North

This painting by John Trumbull shows courageous American colonials facing the might of the red-coated British soldiery at the Battle of Bunker Hill.

everything he could to resist American independence.

The British sent troops to America. In April 1775, they marched to Concord, Massachusetts, to seize an illegal arms cache. The Americans sniped at British troop columns from the dense treeline, forcing them to retreat to Lexington and, finally, back to Boston. Two months later, at the Battle of Bunker Hill, the colonists showed the British that they could hold their own in a pitched battle; the Revolutionary War had begun.

On July 4, 1776, Thomas Jefferson's Declaration of Independence was published. It states, "Whenever any form of government becomes destructive [of the rights of life, liberty, and the pursuit of happiness], it is the right of the people to alter or to abolish it, and to institute new government."

By 1779, most Britons were tired of the war. But George was afraid that stopping the war would set off revolts in other colonies, such as Ireland, so he stubbornly refused to listen to any talk of peace. The British won a number of early victories. In 1781, George Washington, high commander of the American troops, declared, "We are at the end of our tether." But the truth was that the British economy was being ruined by the cost of war. King George had fought with Parliament to end the costly Seven Years' War, but he resisted giving up on the American colonies.

By 1782, despite Washington's concern, the Americans were fighting tenaciously, and many ministers saw the need to end the war. Terms for a general peace were agreed to in 1783. King George, in a fit of despair, drafted a letter of abdication. He felt so deeply that the loss of the American colonies would be a personal failure that he "with much sorrow finds he can be of no further utility to his native country." The letter was never delivered.

4

The Empire in India and the King's Illness

King George believed that the loss of the American colonies would mean the end of British greatness. But the British retained control of the West Indies and of Canada, where their influence had been strengthened by the victory over the French in the Seven Years' War. In a very different part of the world, at the same time that the Revolutionary War was being fought, the British were embarking on another colonial enterprise—India. (The empire in India would become the source of the vast

Although the British were dealt a humiliating defeat in the war with the American revolutionaries, they remained masters of the seas for years to come. This sea power helped the British to found an empire that stretched around the globe.

wealth of Britain's Victorian Age in the 1800s; at the height of this era, Queen Victoria was crowned Empress of India.)

The beginnings of the British Empire in India differed from the settlement of the Americas. In the Americas, the British planted settlements and hoped that they would one day turn a profit. In India, the British East India Company, operating separately from the British government, forged trade links and grew wealthy before India came under government control.

India in the eighteenth century was fragmented, and the colonial powers of France and Britain made alliances with local chieftains to establish trading ports. The British East India Company fought in India against French competition to establish colonies on the East coast of the subcontinent. During the Seven Year's War, the company's own private army was supplemented by government troops. The combined forces were generally victorious against the French. Against hostile Indian tribes, however, the British suffered a few humiliating defeats.

The British East India Company, complete with a private army, preceded the British government's involvement in India. Facets of Indian life captured the imagination of Britons, and many Indian words, such as "mogul" and "pajamas," entered the English language.

The much-hated Surajah Dowlah

In one instance, a local prince named Surajah Dowlah raised a modern army, complete with European guns and gunners, and marched on Calcutta, a rich trading center in northeastern India, to drive out the British. As the Indian army, more than forty thousand strong, neared the city, Europeans and Indians alike fled. One hundred and forty-six Europeans stayed to defend the city.

It was reported that the wantonly cruel Surajah Dowlah defeated them and thrust them into a single prison cell, only 18 feet by 14 feet, 10 inches (5.5 m x 4.5 m). This was during the hottest time of the year in India, and heat, thirst, and fear suffocated the prisoners overnight. When the cell door was swung open in the morning, only twenty-three prisoners were still alive.

The prison was ever after known as the "Black Hole of Calcutta." (A recent study showed that about sixty-four men were detained, not 146; but either way, it was a disaster.)

The Black Hole of Calcutta

A young clerk in the British East India Company, Robert Clive, was called on to avenge the disaster. He had become valuable to the company when revolts broke out. Clive proved to be a genius not only of battle but of administration, and he helped bring large tracts of Indian territory under British control. He was described by William Pitt as a "heaven-born general."

In 1757, Clive retook Calcutta. But revenge on Dowlah's forces came at Plassey, where Clive's forces defeated a larger force with the help of confederates in Dowlah's camp. Dowlah's forces retreated, and he was assassinated a few days later by Indians who were disgusted by his savage cruelty. "The dealings of Surajah Dowlah with the British," wrote one Englishman, "had ensured they would become the next rulers of India."

The horrors of the Black Hole prompted Parliament to demand government intervention in India. In 1773, King George and Lord North backed the Regulating Act, which brought the British government directly into Indian affairs. George III never realized the extent to which the empire in India would enrich Britain. In 1783, when contemplating abdication, he feared that the British Empire was at an end. He could not have been more mistaken.

If George III had abdicated, his son the Prince of Wales would have taken the throne. This may have been one of the reasons that George decided to stay where he was. Though he had many faults, King George III was a man of serious temperament and was absolutely devoted to the kingship. His eldest son, on the other hand, was serious only about satisfying his whims.

As soon as he was old enough to enter society, the prince seemed determined to annoy his father. He gambled, courted women, entertained opportunistic politicians (the "bad men" George had spoken of), and ran up

George Augustus Frederick made it a point of pride as Prince of Wales to oppose and embarrass his father at every opportunity.

enormous debts on extravagant clothes. In what would seem a final insult to his father, the prince sided with the Americans during the American War of Independence.

In 1785, the prince's antics took on a more serious nature. He secretly married a widowed Catholic named Maria Fitzherbert. Under the Act of Settlement, marriage to a Catholic was forbidden in Protestant Britain, and the prince would forfeit his right to rule. Remarkably, the marriage was kept secret from King George and the nation.

The years just after the loss of the colonies were particularly trying for the king. Lord North had asked George to release him from office. "Let me not go to the grave," he said, "with the guilt of having been the ruin of my King and country." After the war, when George felt all was lost, he accepted North's resignation. A new administration was formed by William Pitt's son, known as William Pitt the Younger.

The strain of events in America and the prince's scandalous exhibitions affected King George's health, and by 1788 he was ill. First he complained of physical pains, then he began to mumble incessantly, and soon he was imagining that floods were engulfing London.

George's mind plunged into madness. Removed from London and confined by a straightjacket, he raved day

King George, pursued by attendants and in the throes of his madness, flails around the grounds of Windsor Castle believing that floods were upon them. This image is from the film *The Madness of King George.*

and night, occasionally collapsing from exhaustion. A team of doctors tried fruitlessly to diagnose and cure the king's illness, but all they could agree on was his "entire alienation of mind."

The Prince of Wales held high hopes that his father might die, allowing him to take the throne and end his financial troubles. On one occasion when the prince visited his father, King George sprang from his chair and attempted to strangle his ungrateful heir.

Opposition politicians, friendly with the Prince of Wales, introduced a Regency Bill into Parliament; this bill would make the prince regent, or king in all but name, until his father died. It appeared likely that the Regency Bill would be adopted when, suddenly, George surfaced from his madness. To the astonishment of all, he resumed business as usual.

5

THE FINAL BOUT

King George's madness won for a time the one thing that all of his efforts at just governance could not: affection from his subjects. He began to gain in popularity as the British people reacted with horror to the excesses of the Prince of Wales. Many became proud of his devotion to the government and to his family. Finally, his illness caused a vast outpouring of sympathy.

Never fond of city life, the king spent more and more time at Windsor Castle, a rural residence

northwest of London. At Windsor, George played cards, hunted fox, and strolled through the gardens. He had a way of terrifying his gardeners by firing questions at them; before they could answer, George was barking "What? What?" and then moving on to the next question.

His simple outdoor interests earned the king the nickname "Farmer George" from his subjects, who had finally realized how different he was from his German ancestors. King George also had a lifelong passion for the music of George Frideric Handel. As a youth, George had met the great composer. Handel had remarked, "While that boy lives, my music will never want a protector."

The king's mind was still shaky, however, and his control over the government loosened. He was never again looked on with complete confidence, and many still believed that a regency should be declared. The king was fortunate in his new alliance with William Pitt the

The German composer George Frideric Handel (1685-1759), who had played for George I in Hanover, eventually followed the king to England, where he became a naturalized citizen. He was George III's favorite composer.

Younger. Pitt had enough clout to carry support in Parliament, and the king used his powers to support Pitt's government. The two continued in this fashion for more than seventeen years.

Although George had become less involved in governing, he was not out of the game altogether. Too much was afoot. In France, public opinion had been turning swiftly against the monarchy. During the French Revolution, executioners lopped off the heads of aristocrats amid jubilant cheers in Paris's Place de la Concorde. Much to George's relief, the British did not follow suit. When the British government warned France not to interfere

William Pitt the Younger addresses the House of Commons. As the picture shows, the House of Commons is divided into two sides representing the two opposing parties. Members sitting in the front rows are the most powerful party members, and behind them are the "back benchers," those who hold less popular views.

The execution of the French King Louis XVI at Paris's Place de la Concorde on January 21, 1793, sent a tremor through the remaining royal houses of Europe.

with their monarchy, France responded by declaring war in 1793.

King George involved himself personally in this conflict when it affected Ireland, which was at that time entirely under the control of the British government. The Irish in their own country lived as second-class citizens.

Their laws were made by Protestant British settlers, and their native Gaelic tongue and Catholic religion were discouraged.

Militant groups, such as the United Irishmen (1791), had organized to fight for greater religious freedoms and parliamentary reform. British troops were called in to crush armed resistance, and the Irish rebels turned to France for support. A French force landed in 1798 but was quickly defeated by the British. To calm the situation, Pitt drew up the Act of Union. This joined the parliaments of Ireland and Britain into the United Kingdom. King George consented to this in 1800, and the Irish gained one hundred seats in the House of Commons.

In order for an Irish politician to sit in the House of Commons, however, he was obligated to be a member of the Protestant Church of England, of which the king was head. Catholics were forced to choose between allegiance to the king and allegiance to their faith. In 1801, Pitt attempted to relieve Catholic statesmen of this burden by writing the Catholic Emancipation Bill, which would allow them to serve in Parliament without abandoning Catholicism.

Pitt's bill would probably have gone far in quieting the Irish troubles. But King George was convinced that Catholic emancipation would violate his Coronation

Oath. Had not his Protestant ancestors been brought to Britain to prevent the spread of Catholicism? George's old stubbornness was back. He managed to threaten or bribe members of Parliament until he had enough support to kill the bill. Pitt was forced to resign.

The strain of that political battle brought on another bout of the king's illness. Once more he vanished from public view to wander the halls of Windsor in his long purple nightdress, fighting mad hallucinations. "To deal plainly," George admitted, "I fear I am not in my perfect mind."

The king swung in and out of madness, reviving at times to give some directive to the prime minister or remind the government not to concede too much to the Catholics. It was a slow and painful decline. His attendants often fled as he attempted to rip the hair from their heads. He accused his doctor of sleeping with his wife and at times thought he was married to a different woman.

By 1810, George's illness had taken him firmly into its clutches. The British had to face the unfortunate fact that their king was mad. A new Regency Bill was put

As portrayed in the movie *The Madness of King George,* Charlotte (played by British actress Helen Mirren) comforts the king (played by Nigel Hawthorne) as he realizes that he is not in his "perfect mind."

Napoléon leads French cavalry troops into the Battle of Waterloo in 1815.

forth, and this time it was adopted. The Prince of Wales took the throne on February 5, 1811.

In France, the French Revolution had produced Napoléon Bonaparte, who declared himself Emperor of the French in 1804. His ambitions shook the entire European continent. King George referred to Napoléon's seizure of power as "the impudent overthrow of the monstrous French Republic by a Corsican adventurer." The king himself had drawn up plans to defend Britain should Napoléon carry out his threats of invasion.

But Napoléon turned eastward, where he defeated his Austrian enemies and marched his armies all the way to Russia. The British mobilized and, under the duke of Wellington, defeated Napoléon's armies in the Battle of Waterloo in June 1815.

George knew little of that battle, however, having entirely lost his wits by that time. He had slipped into the foggy and isolated world of his mind. His cheeks had hollowed and his beard had grown long and white. His eyesight had failed, and he filled his lonely hours by playing Handel's music on the harpsichord. His illness was diagnosed at the time as flying gout. Doctors of a later age thought it might have been porphyria, an inherited disease. The nature of his ailment is still debated.

King George had been singularly out of step with his own times. He ruthlessly upheld what he believed to be his sacred duties as king. His devotion was as astounding as his lack of foresight. He lived above all in an age of revolution. The American Revolution, the French Revolution, and the Industrial Revolution all passed his bleary eyes. He resisted them with all his heart. "I will have no innovation in my time," he declared.

In 1820, the king entered his eighty-first year. His body was rapidly deteriorating, and on the night of January 29 he died. In his lifetime, George had succeeded in winning some battles with Parliament, increasing the role of the crown in politics, and earning the affection of his people. In his madness, he was fortunate not to see the contempt with which his son George IV's reign was greeted. The English poet Percy Shelley captured the mood in verse:

An old, mad, despised and dying King,
Princes, the dregs of their dull race, who flow
Through public scorn—mud from a muddy spring—
rulers who neither see nor feel nor know
But leech-like to their fainting country cling.

Parliament in the next years considerably reduced the power of the monarchy through legislation, and King George III was remembered almost entirely for his faults alone, for the loss of the American colonies, and for what was perceived as a tyrannous interference in the British Parliament.

George III preferred Windsor Castle to the bustling life of London. Beset by madness during his last days, Windsor Castle became something of a prison for the moonstruck king.

For More Information

Corzine, Phyllis A. *The French Revolution.* San Diego: Lucent Books, 1995.

Letters from George III to Lord Bute, 1756 to 1766. Edited by Romney Sedgwick. Reprint of 1939 edition. Westport, Conn.: Greenwood Publishing Group, 1981.

Otfinoski, Steven. *Triumph and Tears: The French Revolution.* New York: Facts on File, 1993.

For Advanced Readers

Cannon, John, and Ralph Griffiths. *The Oxford Illustrated History of the British Monarchy.* New York: Oxford University Press, 1989.

Churchill, Winston. *A History of the English Speaking Peoples.* Vol. 3, *The Age of Revolution.* New York: Dodd, Mead, & Co., 1957.

Hibbert, Christopher. *Redcoats and Rebels: The American Revolution through British Eyes.* New York: Avon, 1991.

Pares, Richard. *King George III and the Politicians.* New York: Oxford University Press, 1988.

Movie

The Madness of King George. Starring Nigel Hawthorne and Helen Mirren, this film depicts the bizarre behavior of the king in the throes of his sickness. Directed by Nicholas Hytner. Screenplay by Alan Bennett, based on his play *The Madness of George III.* A Close Call Films Production, Samuel Goldwyn Company in association with Channel Four Films, 1994.

Internet Sites

Due to the changeable nature of the Internet, sites appear and disappear very quickly. Internet addresses must be entered with capital and lowercase letters exactly as they appear.

The Yahoo directory of the World Wide Web is an excellent place to find Internet sites on any topic. The directory is located at:

http://www.yahoo.com

An exhibit in honor of the 250th anniversary of the birth on May 19, 1744, of Sophie Charlotte, Princess of Mecklenburg-Strelitz, and Queen and Consort of King George III has been coded in HTML. It presents an engaging look at the lives of both Charlotte and George and provides links to additional sources of information:

http://www.lib.virginia.edu/exhibits/charlotte/

Many Web sites and search engines provide information and links on broader topics in history. One example is a Web page called History Resources, a guide to a huge variety of history sites:

http://www.liv.ac.uk/~evansjon/humanities/history/history.html

Elizabeth II
1952-

George VI
1936-1952

Edward VIII
1936

George V
1910-1936

House of Windsor

House of Saxe-Coburg-Gotha

George IV
1820-1830

House of Hanover

William III
1689-1702

Mary II
1689-1694

James II
1685-1688

Charles II
1660-1685

Charles I
1625-1649

James I
1603-1625

House of Stuart

Kings and Queens of England and Great Britain with Years of Reign

House of Normandy

The House of Hanover

GEORGE I
(1660-1727)
reign 1714-1727

Augusta of Saxe-Gotha-Altenberg
(1719-1772)

Frederick Louis Prince of Wales
(1707-1751)

GEORGE III
(1738-1820)
reign 1760-1820
(regency declared 1811)

Charlotte of Mecklenburg-Strelitz
(1744-1818)

GEORGE IV
(1762-1830)
reign 1820-1830
(regent 1811-1820)

Caroline of Brunswick-Wolfenbüttel
(1768-1821)

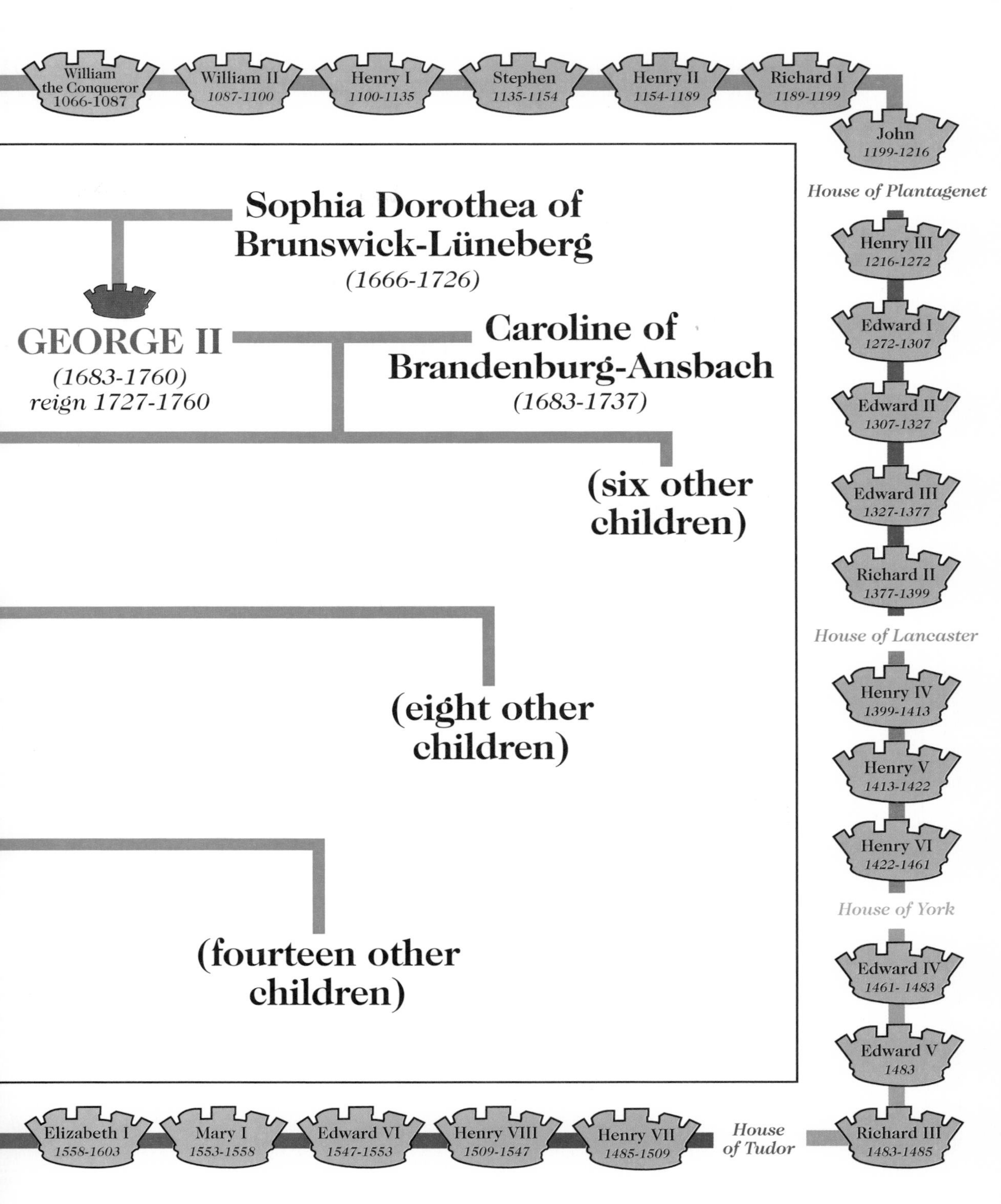
William the Conqueror 1066-1087
William II 1087-1100
Henry I 1100-1135
Stephen 1135-1154
Henry II 1154-1189
Richard I 1189-1199
John 1199-1216
House of Plantagenet
Henry III 1216-1272
Edward I 1272-1307
Edward II 1307-1327
Edward III 1327-1377
Richard II 1377-1399
House of Lancaster
Henry IV 1399-1413
Henry V 1413-1422
Henry VI 1422-1461
House of York
Edward IV 1461- 1483
Edward V 1483
Richard III 1483-1485
House of Tudor
Henry VII 1485-1509
Henry VIII 1509-1547
Edward VI 1547-1553
Mary I 1553-1558
Elizabeth I 1558-1603
Sophia Dorothea of Brunswick-Lüneberg
(1666-1726)
GEORGE II
(1683-1760)
reign 1727-1760
Caroline of Brandenburg-Ansbach
(1683-1737)
(six other children)
(eight other children)
(fourteen other children)

Index

Numbers in *italics* refer to illustrations.

About the Author

Robert Green is a freelance writer who lives in New York City. He is the author of *"Vive la France": The French Resistance during World War II* and biographies of important figures of the ancient world: *Alexander the Great, Cleopatra, Hannibal, Herod the Great, Julius Caesar,* and *Tutankhamun,* all for Franklin Watts. He has also written biographies of Queen Elizabeth I and Queen Elizabeth II.